A New True Book

SONGBIRDS

By Alice K. Flanagan

Subject Consultant
David E. Willard, Ph.D.
Collection Manager of Birds at the Field Museum
of Natural History, Chicago, Illinois

ⓒⅠⓟ Children's Press®
A Division of Grolier Publishing
New York   London   Hong Kong   Sydney
Danbury, Connecticut

The canary is among the most popular of caged songbirds.

I dedicate this book to my grandmother Katherine, whose kindness to birds opened my heart to their song.

PHOTO CREDITS

Animals, Animals — © Breck Kent, 2; © Robert Maier, 4 (left), 9 (right), 41 (top right); © V. I. Anderson, 4 (right); © Gerard Lacz, 6; © Michael and Elvan Habicht, 16; © Roland Mayr, 18; © Nigel Cattlin, 20; © Darek Karp, 24 (bottom); © Tom Edwards, 34; © John Trott, 36 (right); © Patty Murray, 37 (left); © Peter Weimann, 37 (right); © Robert Comport, 39; © Jos Korenromp, 42 (left); © Joe McDonald, 42 (right); © Ralph A. Reinhold, 45 (top); © Francis Lepine, 45 (bottom)

Valan Photos — © Wayne Lankinen, cover, 36 (left), 41 (bottom left and right); © Robert C. Simpson, 9 (top left), 10 (left), 13, 15, 32; © J. R. Page, 9 (bottom), 22, 28; © John Fowler, 10 (right); © Michel Bourque, 21; © Esther Schmidt, 23; © L. McPhee, 24 (top); © John Mitchell, 31; © Jeff Foott, 41 (top left)

Vantage Art — illustration, 27

COVER: American Goldfinch

Project Editor: Dana Rau
Electronic Composition: Biner Design
Photo Research: Flanagan Publishing Services

Library of Congress Cataloging-in-Publication Data

Flanagan, Alice.
  Songbirds / by Alice K. Flanagan.
    p. cm. — (A New true book)
  Includes index.
  Summary: Explains how and why birds sing.
  ISBN 0-516-01095-6
  1. Songbirds—Vocalization—Juvenile literature.
2. Songbirds—Juvenile literature. [1. Birdsongs.
2. Birds. 3. Animal communication.] I. Title.
QL698.5.F58 1996   95-25803
598.8—dc20   CIP
                      AC

CONTENTS

Thrushes, as a family, are among the most gifted singers. They include the song thrush (left), the nightingale, and the American robin (below).

SONGBIRDS

Somewhere, at this very moment, a bird is singing. It may be just outside your window near a feeder. It may be down the street, perched on a roof or a telephone wire.

Perhaps it is flying over an open field, or hiding among the trees near a

Male Australian zebra finches sing beautifully.

lake, or in a forest.
Wherever birds are, they
gift us with their song.

Like humans, all birds use
sounds to communicate.
Most call, chatter, and sing.
Others make more unusual
sounds with their feathers
and beaks called feather
drumming, wing flapping,
and beak hammering.

About five thousand
species of perching birds
have the ability to sing.
These birds are called
songbirds, or "oscines."

CALLS AND SONGS

The short, simple noises birds make are known as calls. Both male and female birds make these sounds throughout the year.

Songbirds have a greater variety of calls than other birds. For each call there is a specific function. Birds use calls to communicate with a mate or beg for food.

(Above left) A young Carolina wren calls to a parent for food. (Above right) A European chaffinch gives one kind of call when it sees a hawk perched in a nearby tree and another when the hawk takes flight. (Bottom) The house sparrow has eleven different calls.

Contact calls tell young birds where parents are. Calls in flight or on the ground keep members of

A song sparrow (left) and chipping sparrow (right)

a group in touch with each other. Alarm calls scold or scare away intruders or warn other birds that a predator is near. Distress calls signal that a bird is in danger or captured by a predator.

Over time, calls developed into songs. They became longer and more complex. They took on a different meaning. Male birds used them during the breeding season.

Among songbirds, the type and quality of song vary. The song sparrow, for example, has many variations of its song, while the chipping sparrow repeats one song over and over. Some birds sing for only two or three seconds. Others sing for several minutes at a time. Some birds sing only at certain times of the year or during certain times of the day. The red-eyed

The red-eyed vireo feeds on insects in the forests of North America. It is sometimes called a "greenlef," because of its greenish color.

vireo holds the record for the most songs sung in one day — more than 22,000!

WHY BIRDS SING

Close observations of birds in the wild show that they sing for several reasons. The most important reason is to protect territory. During the breeding season, male birds sing to inform other birds of the territory they have claimed for their nests. The song is meant to keep out intruders

Cardinals often sing more frequently after their offspring have left the nest. It may be that, with more cardinals spread throughout the territory, there is more to defend.

while nesting and feeding are taking place.

Birds regularly travel throughout their territory to protect it. They stop at favorite singing spots where

The voice of the beautiful male blue jay is loud and harsh.
In fall and winter, it sounds like it is calling "Thief!" "Thief!"

they break into song. A
male sings loudly and often
when he wants to tell rival
males that the territory he is

protecting is wide. This message must be loud enough to reach them. To frighten away intruders, birds often combine song with a type of visual display — such as ruffling their feathers or raising their tails.

After establishing a territory, a male looks for a mate. This is another reason birds sing. To attract a mate, a male shows off his best. He sings and postures to get a female's attention. His "love song" tells her that he is of the same species and interested in mating. His movements often excite the female. Usually, the most

A sedge warbler's song is long and complicated when it is courting females. After it finds a mate, it stops singing.

attractive males with the most highly developed displays have the best chance of mating and reproducing.

Many people who live closely with songbirds and study their behavior believe that some species sing when they feel safe and well fed in their territory. But no one has proved that birds can express feeling in song. What do you think?

Listen to the sound of a beautiful song coming from a bird perched on a rooftop or a trio hidden in a tree. Think about why and how they change parts of their song as they sing. Perhaps one day our knowledge of birds will include more reasons why birds sing.

The long, loud singing of English male robins is actually a contest for possession of territory. The loudest and best singer eventually occupies the territory.

A common grackle singing at sunset

WHERE BIRDS SING

Birds usually choose a prominent place to sing. It may be at the top of a tall tree, a fence, or a bush. Sometimes it is a telephone pole or a tall building. Usually, the spot is at the edge of a bird's territory.

21

The nest is well in sight but far enough away so that the singing will not attract a predator to it. Ideally, the song post is at a height from which the

Male red-winged blackbirds who have the most impressive songs usually have the best territories.

bird can see a predator coming. Also, it is close enough to tree cover in case it must escape. Song posts that are well hidden allow birds to sing longer

Meadow larks live in grassy fields, meadows, and marshes. Their song is one of the first songs we hear in spring.

A chestnut-colored longspur (left) and a skylark (below)

without the threat of being caught by a predator. The grasshopper warbler, which stays well hidden, sometimes sings for more than two minutes.

Birds often try out several song posts before deciding which ones are the safest and will allow their song to reach the farthest. Some birds do not use song posts at all. Larks, longspurs, and pipits sing their songs while in flight.

HOW BIRDS SING

Songbirds have a highly developed organ for making sounds. This tiny organ is called the syrinx. It is at the base of the throat, or trachea. Inside the syrinx are thin sheets of skin, called membranes. They vibrate when air, coming from the lungs, passes over them. There are muscles

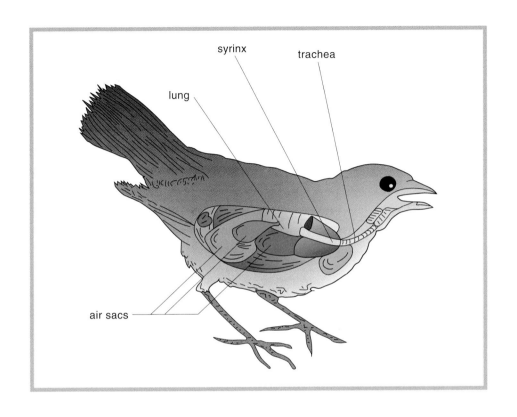

attached to the syrinx. As
they tighten and relax,
different sounds are made.
Some birds have none of
these muscles. Others

have only one or two pairs
of muscles. Songbirds can
have up to nine pairs.

Some people compare
what happens to a bird's
syrinx to a balloon filled
with air. When the neck of

A song sparrow

the balloon is stretched, air escapes. The more the balloon is stretched the higher the sound will be.

An air sac that surrounds the syrinx also affects the kinds of sounds birds make. When filled with air, the air sac puts pressure on the syrinx and changes the sound.

The length and width of the trachea also affect sound. A short, narrow trachea produces a higher sound than a short, wide one.

LEARNING TO SING

When you were born, you did not know how to talk. You had to learn language. Young birds are like that, too. They must learn the songs of their parents.

All birds are born with an ability to communicate. But their ability to sing a particular song is learned little by little. It must be

At birth, robins cannot sing. The only sounds they make are begging calls for food.

learned from other adult birds.

The age at which a bird sings varies. Young song sparrows may start to sing as early as their fourteenth day of life. But for other birds it takes a longer period of time.

A young bird plays with sounds in infancy. Later, the sounds become phrases. Finally, after much practice imitating adult birds, most nestlings learn

In infancy, a young robin will practice sounds it hears from the adults in its family.

the full song of their species. After a young bird sets itself up in a territory, it perfects its song. By listening to more mature birds and experimenting on its own, a young bird makes the species' song its own.

Each bird sings the song of its species, but does it in its own way. It has its own vocal characteristics, which its mate can recognize.

Recognizing the voice of a specific bird is important, especially in large

When a robin has learned the full song of its species, it will gradually perfect it.

communities, or colonies, of birds. Among thousands of calling birds, mates have to be able to recognize each other by voice. Offspring need to be able to find their parents, too.

IMITATING SONG

As well as learning their own songs, many birds borrow or imitate the songs of other species. This is called mimicry. The North American mockingbird is a great imitator. It can mimic the calls and songs of just about all the birds near its territory. European

An adult mockingbird (left) and
a fledging taking a bath (right)

marsh warblers are known to
mimic as many as one
hundred species, some of
them from Africa, where marsh
warblers spend the winter.

In Australia, lyrebirds are the best mimics. In Great Britain, the wheatear, jay, and red-backed shrike have these abilities. Catbirds, starlings, and white-eyed vireos also reproduce the songs of other birds.

A superb lyrebird (left) and a gray catbird (right)

A white-eyed vireo

Why do birds mimic?
No one knows for sure.
Perhaps male birds imitate
the songs of other birds to
increase the number and

variety of songs they can sing to attract females. Or, they may be simply showing their ability to learn and to communicate.

A superb starling

DUETS AND GROUP SINGING

Although most songs are sung by males, females in some species are known to sing. Female American robins, mockingbirds, and white-crowned sparrows sing when helping to defend their territories. Among other species, females use songs to communicate with their mates. This is true of the bullfinch, crossbill, and some vireos.

White-crowned sparrows (above left),
a pair of bullfinches (above right), and
red crossbills (bottom left and right)

Marsh warbler mates mimic each other. The females learn the flight calls and songs of their mates so

The marsh warbler (left) and the black-headed grosbeak (right) are both fine mimics.

that they can find each other. They sing as a duet. Although both know the entire song, each sings only one part of it. The male usually starts the song, and the female sings the final part.

Some female tropical bush-shrikes sing regularly with the males in very synchronized duets. A mated pair of black-headed gonolek in Africa sing so perfectly together that their song sounds as though it came from a single bird.

Linnets and goldfinches are known to sing in groups. Some even sing as trios or quartets — each joining in with split-second timing.

Songbirds are musicians. Whether they are singing alone or as part of a duet or a group, their songs are unique. Each bird has its own personality and its own way of singing a song that brings music and beauty to our daily lives.

The goldfinch is often called a wild canary because of its lovely song. It likes company and often gathers in small groups.

GLOSSARY

ability (a-BIL-it-ee) — natural talent or skill

breed (BREED) — to produce or increase by reproduction

colony (KAH-luh-nee) — a group of living things of one kind living together

communicate (kuh-MYOO-nuh-kayt) — to exchange information

defend (di-FEND) — to protect from danger or attack

distress (dis-TRES) — danger

duet (doo-ET) — two performers singing together

establish (es-TAB-lish) — to bring into being

experiment (ik-SPEHR-uh-muhnt) — to test something; to find out more about it

infancy (IN-fan-see) — early childhood

intruder (in-TROOD-er) — one who forces himself in

mate (MAYT) — a partner

mature (ma-TOOR) — fully grown or developed

membrane (MEM-brayn) — a thin layer of animal or plant tissue

mimicry (MIH-mih-kree) — the process of imitating

nestling (NEST-ling) — a young bird not yet able to leave the nest

observation (ob-zer-VAY-shun) — the study of a particular thing

offspring (AWF-spring) — the young of an animal

oscines (AH-sins) — songbirds

posture (PAHS-chuhr) — to position the body a certain way

predator (PRED-at-ur) — an animal that kills and eats other animals

prominent (PRAH-muh-nuhnt) — attracting attention

quartet (kwawr-TEHT) — four performers singing together

reproduce (ree-pruh-DYOOS) — to produce another living thing of the same kind

rival (RY-vuhl) — an enemy

species (SPEE-sheez) — animals that form a distinct group made up of related individuals

synchronize (SIN-kruh-nyz) — to happen at the same time

syrinx (SIR-inks) — a highly developed organ for making sounds

territory (TEHR-uh-tohr-ee) — a geographical area belonging to an individual or group

threat (THRET) — a showing of an intention to do harm

trachea (TRAY-kee-uh) — the tube that is used for breathing

trio (TREE-oh) — three performers singing together

vibrate (VY-brayt) — to swing back and forth very fast

vocal (VO-kuhl) — relating to the voice

INDEX

(**Boldface** numbers indicate illustrations.)

ABOUT THE AUTHOR

Alice K. Flanagan is a freelance writer and bird advocate. She considers her strong interest in birds, and a feeling of kinship with them, a symbol of her independence and freedom as a writer. She enjoys writing, especially for children. "The experience of writing," she says, "is like opening a door for a caged bird, knowing you are the bird flying gloriously away."

Ms. Flanagan lives with her husband in Chicago, Illinois, where they take great pleasure in watching their backyard birds.